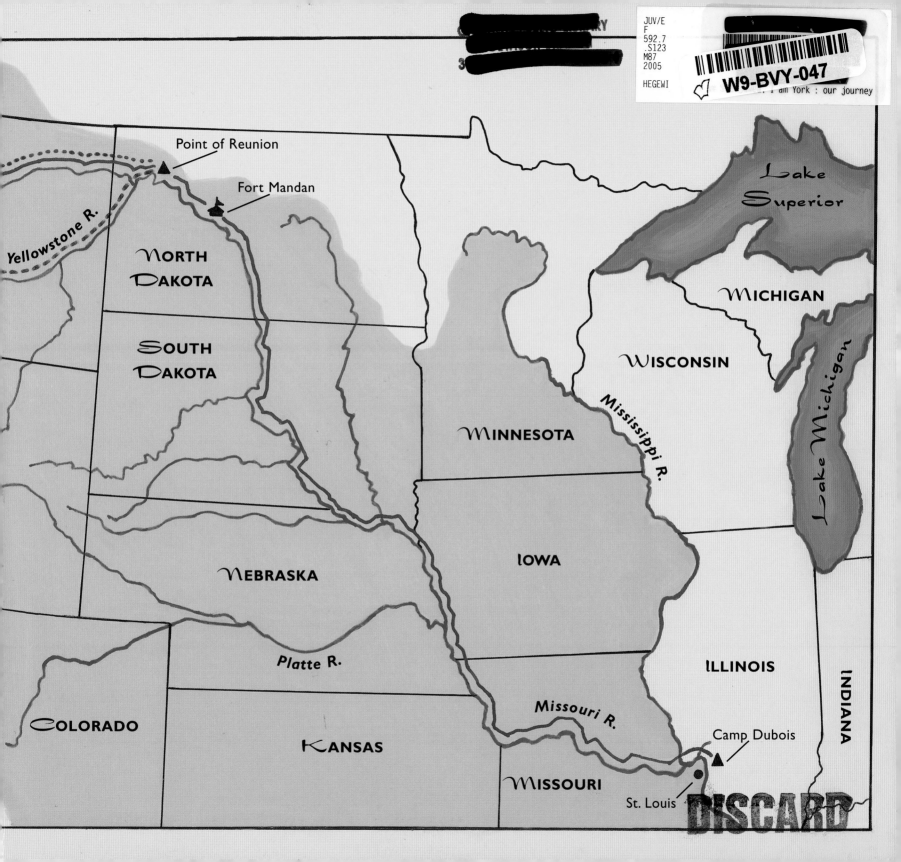

am York : our journey

Point of Reunion

Fort Mandan

Yellowstone R.

Lake Superior

NORTH DAKOTA

SOUTH DAKOTA

MICHIGAN

WISCONSIN

MINNESOTA

Mississippi R.

IOWA

Lake Michigan

NEBRASKA

Platte R.

ILLINOIS

INDIANA

COLORADO

Missouri R.

KANSAS

Camp Dubois

MISSOURI

St. Louis

I Am Sacajawea, I Am York

Our Journey West with Lewis and Clark

Claire Rudolf Murphy

Illustrations by Higgins Bond

Walker & Company ✸ New York

They call me Sacagawea, Bird Woman, but my parents named me *Sacajawea*, one who carries a burden. The Hidatsa of the Great Plains took me far away from my Lemhi Shoshone people when I was only a girl of twelve snows. I worked in their fields until they sold me to Charbonneau, a French Canadian trader who lived in their village. Now, in the time of falling leaves, a baby stirs inside me as I watch huge boats approach. Many men with faces paler than ashes, one with skin like brown soil, and a dog as big as a baby buffalo land on our shores.

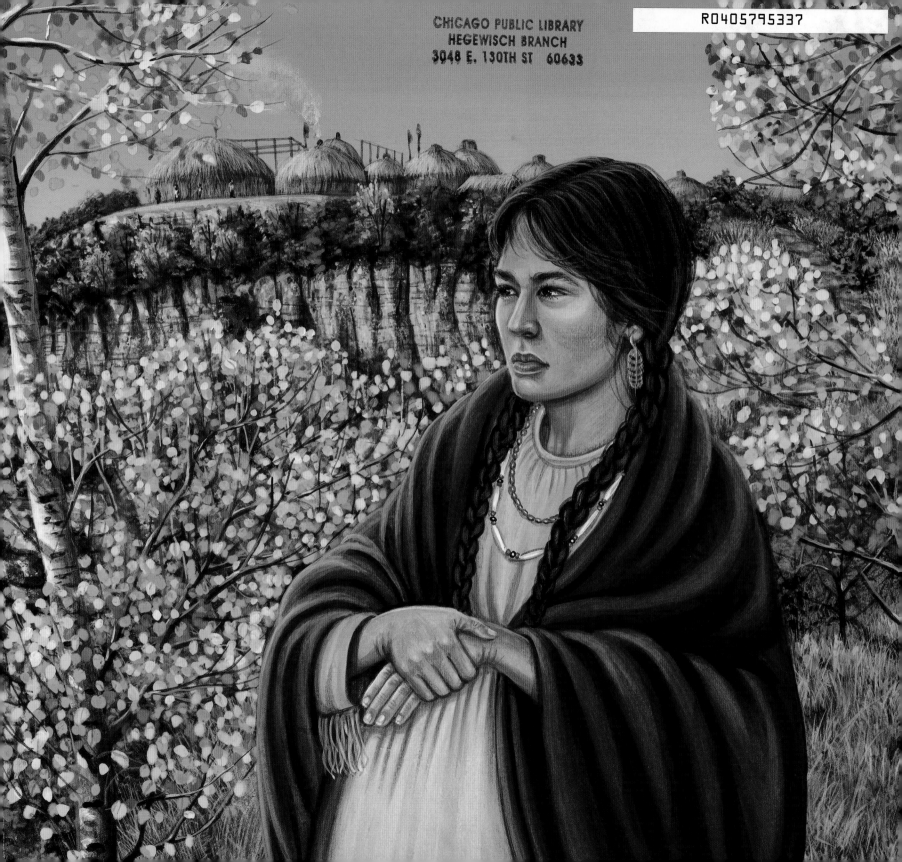

They call me York, after my pappy, Old York, and the York River. On the plantation in Kentucky, Cap'n Clark and I used to play in the fields and go fishing. In my twelfth summer Master moved me into the big house and gave me to his son. I've been by Cap'n's side ever since. On this long journey west to find a route to the Pacific Ocean, I am the only black man.

The children chase the man called York and try to rub off his earth-colored skin. All the people clap when the fiddles play and he kicks and twirls round the campfire. I have never seen such a man as this. But I am glad that he and the dog called Seaman will stay the winter.

One bone-cold day Charbonneau brings his Indian wife to our fort. Cap'n Lewis asks her, "Will you help us buy horses from your Shoshone people? We need them to cross the Rocky Mountains." Sacajawea looks down at her swelling belly, worry on her face. Charbonneau grunts and shakes her shoulders. She nods. She will come with us.

My son was born when the snows were still high. Charbonneau calls him Jean Baptiste. I call him Pompy, the Shoshone word for hair, since he has so much of it. When the green leaves bud, and the big river Missouri flows free, we depart in the white chiefs' canoes.

I am the only woman, Pompy the only child, on this journey. As we travel along, York swats the mosquitoes away and sings my son to sleep.

Sacajawea is a smart woman. She collects prairie turnips and wild onions to cook with the game we have hunted. Charbonneau is a cowardly man. One day a strong gust of wind blows. Charbonneau panics and almost tips over Cap'n's boat. Quicker than ten men, Sacajawea leans over the side of the boat and snatches supplies and the captain's journals out of the swirling water.

As we travel the river, coyote, elk, big-horn sheep, and thousands of buffalo travel the land. My people would never hunger with this plentiful food. When darkness falls, we sleep while Seaman stands watch for the fearsome grizzly bear.

One evening Seaman's barking pierces the air when a large buffalo bull thunders into camp. York and the soldiers mount their guns, and Pompy and I burrow up like rabbits. Good fortune. Seaman heads the bull into the river and saves us all.

For days we carry big loads around the five roaring falls, seventeen miles of back-breaking work. Finally we return the boats to the waters of the Missouri. We pole up the river, day after day. Every morning Cap'n Lewis asks, "Where are your people, Sacajawea?" She only shakes her head.

One day we approach an Indian camp and Sacajawea cries, "A-hi-ee! A-hi-ee!" When she hears the chief's voice, she runs to him. They cling together like a tobacco leaf to its stalk. Sacajawea has found her family. I miss mine back home.

My brother Cameahwait still lives and he is chief! I call out, "Brother, I am Sacajawea, your sister." I finally stop crying and ask my brother if he will sell horses to the captains. "Sister, we need guns to hunt the buffalo," he tells me. But the captains have no guns to trade.

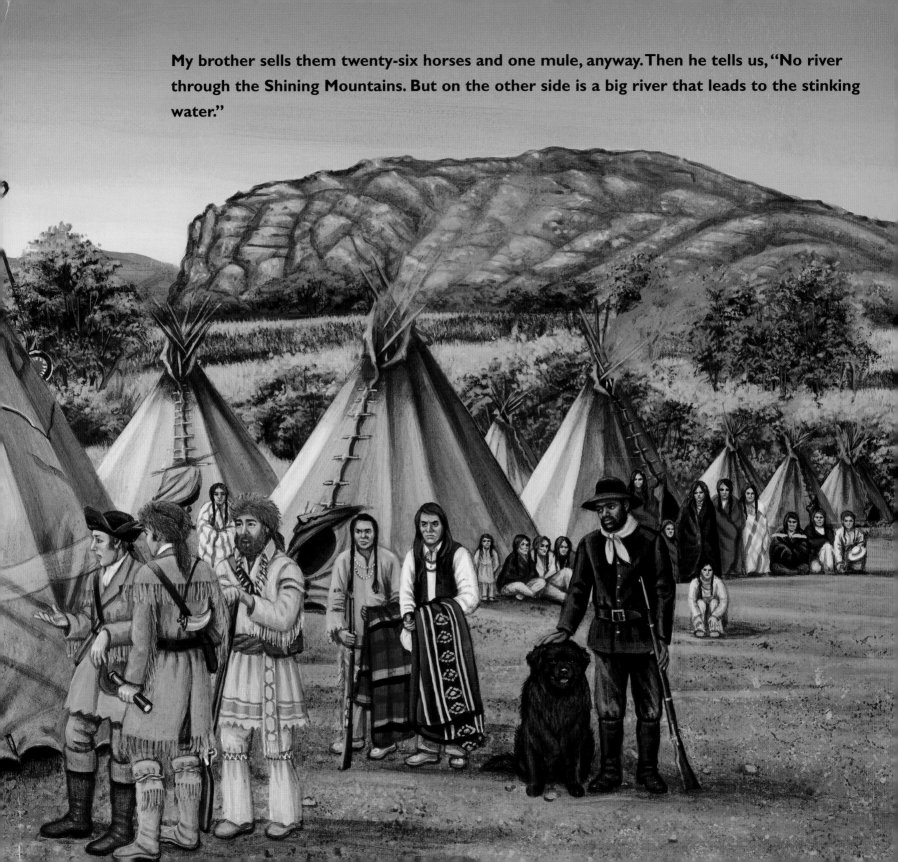

My brother sells them twenty-six horses and one mule, anyway. Then he tells us, "No river through the Shining Mountains. But on the other side is a big river that leads to the stinking water."

Sacajawea belongs to Charbonneau, like I belong to Cap'n. She and Pompy travel with us into the mountains through rain, hail, and snow. I long for the warm breezes and rolling hills of Kentucky. But Sacajawea does not complain, and Pompy barely whimpers. We cannot find game and grow so hungry that Cap'n commands us to shoot one of the colts. Sacajawea refuses to eat the horse meat. She and Pompy survive only on the roots and berries she digs up.

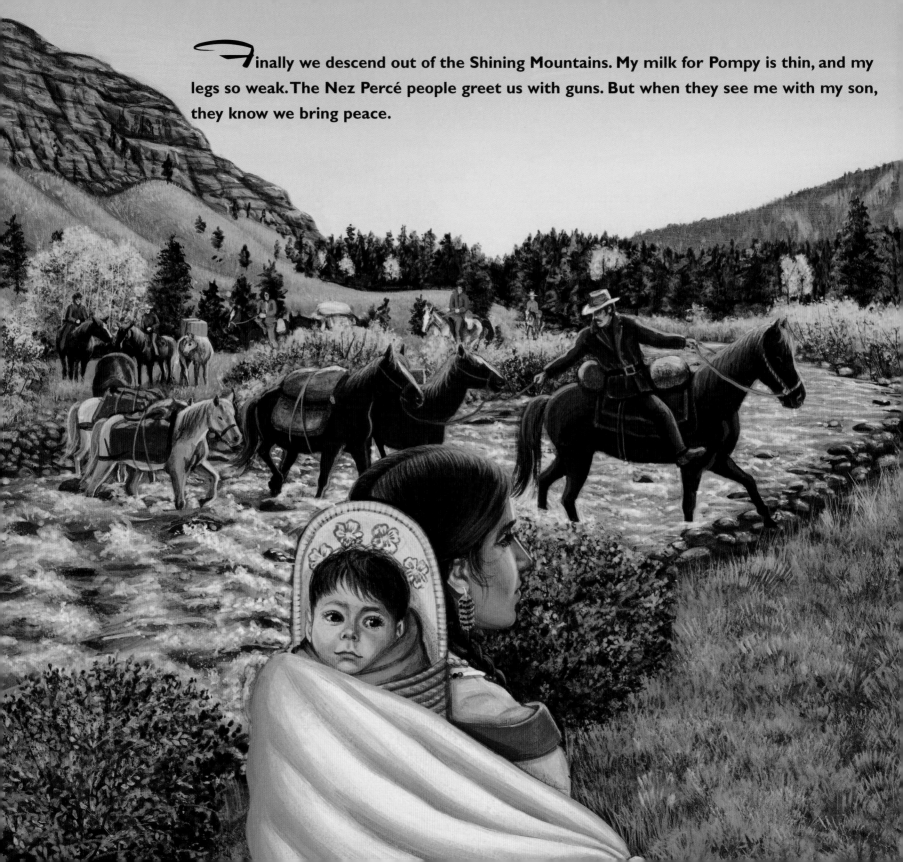

Finally we descend out of the Shining Mountains. My milk for Pompy is thin, and my legs so weak. The Nez Percé people greet us with guns. But when they see me with my son, they know we bring peace.

Still they circle around York, yelling, "Burnt Man! Burnt Man!" and pet him like a dog. They do not know yet that under his dark skin his heart beats like ours.

*T*he Indians feed us camas roots and salmon, Chinook with rosy pink flesh. I eat until my stomach almost bursts. After we rest, the Nez Percé show us how to dig out canoes from huge Ponderosa pine trees. Chief Twisted Hair draws a map on white elk skin, naming the Clearwater, Snake, and Columbia, rivers we must travel before we reach the ocean.

The salmon are so thick we cannot dip an oar in the river without striking a silvery back. Along these shores many different tribes live. They fish with nets and celebrate their catches with song and drum. The sun shines down on us until we reach treacherous rapids, one after another. We must survive so we can reach the Big Water that never ends.

Day and night the rain pours down. Finally we reach the Pacific Ocean. Hallelujah! Cap'n Lewis asks each soldier and Charbonneau where to build our winter fort. He records their votes in his book. Then my cap'n taps my shoulder. He wants me, a slave, to vote? My heart thumps! He points to Sacajawea, too. I smile at her. I am York. She is Sacajawea. For this one moment we are free.

Afterword

The incidents in this story all come from recorded details in the Lewis and Clark journals. The vote to decide the location of the winter camp is the first record of an African American man and a Native American woman being allowed to participate in a vote. It took place sixty years before the slaves were freed and more than one hundred years before Indians or women were given the right to vote.

The expedition's return journey, starting in March 1806, was equally challenging. On August 14, 1806, they arrived at Fort Mandan, North Dakota, where Sacajawea, Charbonneau, and Pompy left the expedition. Charbonneau was paid $500 for his services. Sacajawea received nothing.

Lewis and Clark's eight-thousand-mile journey ended in St. Louis, Missouri, on September 23, 1806. Clark later wrote, "Sacajawea has been of great service to me as a pilot through this country." No compliments  were recorded about York, and he, too, received no payment. After the expedition, York requested his freedom so that he could join his wife, a slave, in Kentucky. But Clark didn't free him for several more years. Most historians and Sacajawea's own Lemhi Shoshone people believe that she died of a fever on December 20, 1812, at Fort Manuel, South Dakota. But a few historians contend that she traveled around the West for seventy-two more years and spent her final years on the Wind River Reservation in Wyoming until her death in April 1884. More monuments, schools, rivers, lakes, and parks are dedicated to Sacajawea than to any other woman in American history. The golden dollar coin features her image with Pompy on her back. When Pompy was older, he lived in St. Louis with Captain Clark and attended school.

Clark named a tributary of the Yellowstone River (in Montana) Dry Creek York, in honor of his slave. But until recently, York's contributions to the Corps of Discovery have been largely overlooked. Earlier writings about the expedition portrayed him as a lazy buffoon. Yet such a man could not have survived the journey or contribute as he did. After obtaining his freedom, York drove a freight wagon in Kentucky and Tennessee. Most historians believe York died of cholera in Tennessee around 1832. But some Indian tribes claim to have seen him years later in the West, living as an honored chief of the Crow Indians.

For Further Reading

Blumberg, Rhoda. *The Incredible Journey of Lewis & Clark*. New York: HarperTrophy, 1995.

————. *York's Adventures with Lewis and Clark: An African-American's Part in the Great Expedition*. New York: HarperCollins, 2003.

Calvert, Patricia. *Great Lives: The American Frontier*. New York: Atheneum, 1997.

Cobblestone. *"The Lewis and Clark Expedition, 1804–1806."* September 1980. Entire magazine.

Erdrich, Liselotte. *Sacagawea*. Minneapolis: Carolrhoda Books, 2003.

Hunsaker, Joyce Badgley. *They Call Me Sacagawea*. Guilford, CT: Globe Pequot Press, 2003.

Lourie, Peter. *On the Trail of Sacagawea*. Honesdale, PA: Boyds Mills Press, 2001.

Myers, Laurie. *Lewis and Clark and Me: A Dog's Tale*. New York: Henry Holt, 2002.

Patent, Dorothy Hinshaw. *The Lewis and Clark Trail: Then and Now*. New York: Dutton, 2002.

Roop, Connie and Peter. *Girl of the Shining Mountains: Sacagawea's Story*. New York: Hyperion Press, 1999.

————. *Off the Map: The Journals of Lewis and Clark*. New York: Walker & Company, 1993.

St. George, Judith. *Sacagawea*. New York: Philomel Books, 1997.

Thomasma, Kenneth. *The Truth About Sacagawea*. Jackson, WY: Grandview Publishing Company, 1997.

Van Steenwyk, Elizabeth. *My Name Is York*. Flagstaff, AZ: Rising Moon, 1997.

Selected Web Sites:

http://www.lewisandclarktrail.com/ (relive the adventure)

http://www.nps.gov/lecl/ (information about the trail from the National Park Service)

http://www.nationalgeographic.com/features/97/west/main.html (program for kids)

http://www.lewisandclark.com/ (travelers' guide to the trail)

http://www.lcarchive.org/fulllist.html (links to every site on the World Wide Web concerning the Lewis and Clark expedition)

Additional Sources

Betts, Robert B. *In Search of York.* Rev. ed. Boulder: University Press of Colorado, 2002.

DeVoto, Bernard. *The Journals of Lewis and Clark.* Boston: Houghton Mifflin, 1953.

Fifer, Barbara, and Vicky Soderberg. *Along the Trail with Lewis and Clark.* 2nd ed. Helena, MT: Farcountry Press, 2002.

Hunsaker, Joyce Badgley. *Sacagawea Speaks: Beyond the Shining Mountains with Lewis and Clark.* Guilford, CT: Globe Pequot Press, 2001

A Note on Pronunciations

Sacajawea (Sah-kah-ja-wee-ah) was given her name at the age of three by her Lemhi Shoshone people. *Sacajawea* means "one who carries a burden." A *wea* is a basket the girls and women carried on their backs to hold grasses. *Sacaja* means "one who carries." The origin of Sacajawea's name has been passed down through Lemhi Shoshone oral history.

The Hidatsa Indians who kidnapped Sacajawea at the age of twelve pronounced her name Sacagawea (Sah-KAH-gah-WEE-ah). In their language it meant Bird Woman or Crow Woman.

The pronunciation and spelling of Sacajawea's name have caused great confusion over the centuries because of the many and varied phonetic spellings Lewis and Clark used in their journals. Some of them include Sakakawea (Tsa-KAH-kah-WEE-ah), Sah-KAH-joo-ah, and Sah-cawg-a-way-ah. Conversations between Sacajawea and Lewis and Clark had to be translated from English to French to the Hidatsa language, and this compounded the confusion.

For the descendants of Sacajawea and York, and for

Teri Sloat—writer, illustrator, and friend—who helped me grasp the vision for this story.

—C. R. M.

To Tauhearah Muhammed, with love. Her journey is just beginning.

—H. B.

Special thanks to:

Emma and Rozina George, Lemhi Shoshone great-great-great-grandnieces of Sacajawea, for reviewing this manuscript for accuracy; Joyce Badgley Hunsaker; Dr. Darrell Millner, Black Studies Department, Portland State University; Pat Calvert; ranger John Phillips of the Pompey's Pillar Monument; my writing group: Mary Cronk Farrell, Mary Douthit, Meghan Nuttall Sayres; publisher Emily Easton; associate editor Beth Marhoffer; and agent Liza Voges for believing in this book; and finally, my husband and children, who keep me sane.

Text copyright © 2005 by Claire Rudolf Murphy
Illustrations copyright © 2005 by Higgins Bond

First published in the United States of America in 2005 by
Walker Publishing Company, Inc.

Published simultaneously in Canada by Fitzhenry and Whiteside, Markham, Ontario L3R 4T8

For information about permission to reproduce selections from this book, write to
Permissions, Walker & Company, 104 Fifth Avenue, New York, New York 10011

Library of Congress Cataloging-in-Publication Data
available upon request
ISBN 0-8027-8919-6 (hardcover)
ISBN 0-8027-8921-8 (reinforced)

The artist used acrylics on illustration board to create the illustrations for this book.

Book design by Victoria Allen

Visit Walker & Company's Web site at www.walkeryoungreaders.com

Printed in Hong Kong

10 9 8 7 6 5 4 3 2 1

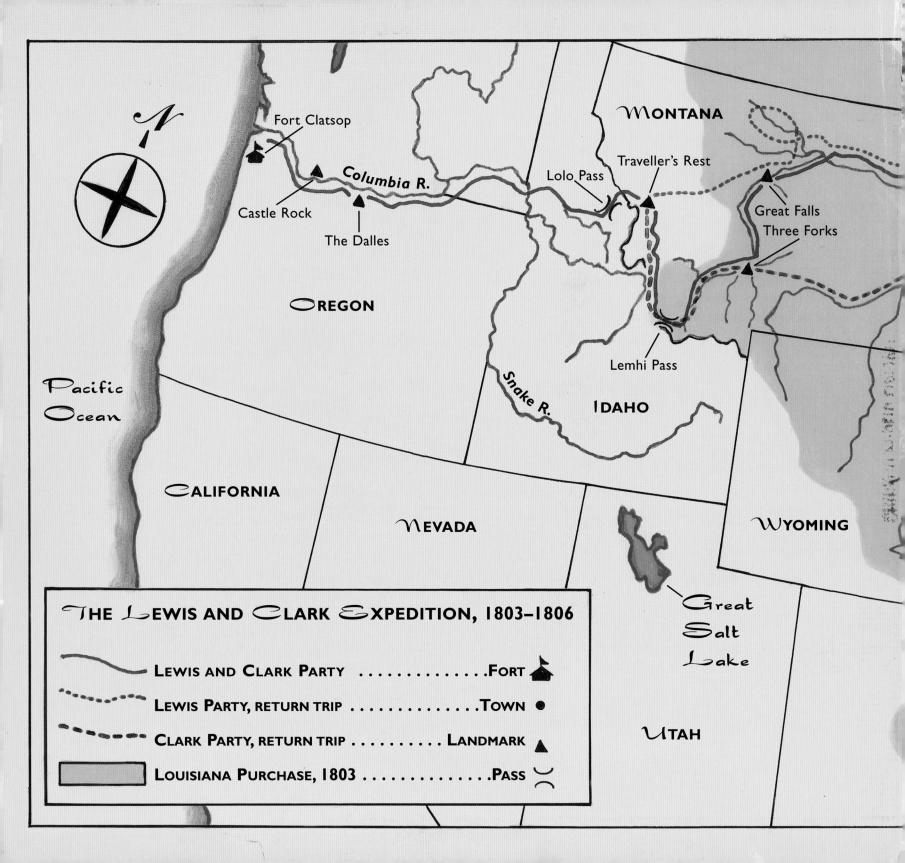

Fort Clatsop

Castle Rock

The Dalles

Columbia R.

MONTANA

Lolo Pass

Traveller's Rest

Great Falls
Three Forks

OREGON

Lemhi Pass

Pacific
Ocean

Snake R.

IDAHO

CALIFORNIA

NEVADA

WYOMING

Great
Salt
Lake

UTAH

THE LEWIS AND CLARK EXPEDITION, 1803–1806

LEWIS AND CLARK PARTY . . . . FORT

LEWIS PARTY, RETURN TRIP . . . . TOWN ●

CLARK PARTY, RETURN TRIP . . . . LANDMARK ▲

LOUISIANA PURCHASE, 1803 . . . . PASS)(